# Looking into the Mind of a Lost but Found Soul

Dwight Mcgarrah Sr

PAGE PUBLISHING, INC.
New York, NY

First originally published by Page Publishing, Inc. 2019

ISBN 978-1-64462-000-7 (Paperback)
ISBN 978-1-64462-001-4 (Digital)

Printed in the United States of America

# DEDICATION

Everything that I was able to overcome came from my father, who art in heaven, the Lord our savior. My endurance came from my dad, James McGarrah. My strength for this book came from my friend and girl Felice Leach. My inspiration came from my mother, Bertha Gibson McGarrah.

I dedicate this book to Ms. Thesba Lewis, Ms. Joyce Leach, Ms. Margaret Bell, Ms. Martha Carter, Ms. Gladys Smith, Ms. Audrey Williams, Ms. Carmen Bachelor, and Ms. Rose Harris.

Why are so many people so rebellious and afraid of the truth? If sometimes you feel an emptiness in your life, it's because you haven't let God in.

———❦———

Beware.

Hey, everyone who is truly a believer—beware, Satan is very crafty. He preys on the weak.

He has many disguises. He can pretend to be your best friend and want the best for you when all the time he loves when you're down!

They pretend to reach their hand to you when you're drowning but it's all a front; when you're underwater looking up, you see the hand and it looks as though they're reaching for you because it's blurry and you're struggling. But in reality, they're just putting it out there. If you reach for it, they're actually pulling it away, but you won't be able to tell because it's blurry and you're struggling.

They will smile in your face and try to separate you from those who love you so they can break you down and steal the soul from one of God's children, but if you truly believe, just when all looks lost and you are at your weakest point, God will rescue you and show you that you have a purpose and remind you to be you. That's why he made you *you* and everyone else *them*. Always believe in God first and yourself.

12/1/17

Dear Lord,

The more I put my trust in you the more you reveal to me.
I feel the pain I caused my parents.
Two people that didn't deserve what I was giving them.
I talk so much about everything of no value.
From my young days, when I started experiencing life, my
mother was a package full of ambition, principles, and God's spirit.
My dad was a complete man.
Me, I was a spoiled brat who got everything materialistic.
Me, looking at things in a selfish way always saying they didn't give
me love and attention when maybe I wanted too much.
My mom taught school and ran Sunday school while doing
her sorority to try and open new doors for me. Also, every year, she
took risks driving, catching a bus or a train to go see her mother
in Georgia while my dad stayed back to protect what he worked
hard for.
Everything they tried to show me I went against.
I personally witnessed pure prejudice: racism, hate, bullying,
murder, misdirection (if you don't stand for something, you'll fall
for anything).
Because God allows me to make choices, I got to see the
darkness and the light, and I chose the light.
Ninety percent really is about the money. Thank God for
that real 10 percent.

You know, if I lived in a cardboard box I wonder how many friends I'd have, how many people would call me.

If I didn't have anything to give, how many people would say uncle, brother, or whatever Mac?

Who would invite me into their home? Who would offer me a meal? A few people fo sho, probably mostly strangers.

My actions are questioned. My blessings are not.

So let me be me and you be you.

I'm getting back to the direction I'm supposed to be going. These street people are too scandalous for me. I want to stay alive and free. What about you?

I started doubting myself.

Now, I think I'm unstoppable with God by my side.

Good mornin', y'all.

To me, life is like a maze and a puzzle together.

It's like, as you're going through this maze, you also have to be putting this puzzle together, seeing what fits, or thinking, Does this piece even belong to this puzzle?

While going through this maze trying to take the right path to get out, sometimes it overwhelms you, and you get confused and frustrated, and you don't know what piece fits or what path to take.

That's when you *whooo-saaa* humble and pray, but you must truly believe, or you will stay stuck.

So follow your heart and stick to the real laws.

God laws.

Follow the real principles: love, honor, humility, respect, loyalty, and keeping your word.

And you should be okay. Doing what you're supposed to always has better results. And stop lying.

4/13/16

Good mornin'.

As the saying goes, you live and you learn.

I was moving so fast. I was learning but not using it wisely and briefly.

I couldn't slow down because I had to save the world also while I was destroying it.

Every day is a struggle, and if you add bullshit to it.

Such as you're getting evicted, you've lost your job, your girl, and damn near your mind. Now the choice comes: should I straighten up stop smoking and drinking, clean myself up, and keep a clear head, or should I get high more and as much as I can to stay in this false world and feel sorry for myself and blame others for my failures?

Which way is up?

Which one of these is the easy way out?

Think about this carefully.

The devil wants you to believe God doesn't hear you.

Believe me, God hears you.

Good mornin', world.

To me, one of the hardest jobs for God's soldiers is to save the soul of someone that has a contract with the devil.

He tries his best not to leave any loopholes.

He has had an infinite amount of time to dot each i and cross each t.

See, God's soldiers know law also. Always remember that only God is perfect, so no matter how hard the devil tries, there is always a loophole in his contract when you give it to God.

Just remember it's easy to get in trouble and hard to get out.

5/7/18

Good mornin', world.

We always speak about putting ourselves in other people's shoes. Have we ever tried to put ourselves in Jesus' shoes?

It's probably impossible to even fathom that thought. We sometimes overlook what God has and is doing for us. Imagine walking around trying to save the same people trying to kill you.

Imagine everyone you trust turning on you.

Just imagine.

Imagine working sun up to sun down for a cup of water and a piece of bread.

Hoping someone doesn't come rape your wife and children and there's nothing you can do.

Then the same person you have to call master so you won't get beaten.

Just imagine.

And we think we have problems.

Hello.

You know, walking with the Lord is the greatest feeling you can have.

He takes away all stress and doubt; you know you have the greatest bodyguard possible. You get so confident, it seems as though you're cocky and arrogant, but you're really humble.

Being humble doesn't mean weak. The meek shall inherit the Earth, not the weak, someone told me.

God can't have weak soldiers. The devil is always looking for that weak point.

Always stand firm in what you believe as long as it makes sense.

To me, learning to be humble as a true leader is hard, but once they learn humility in the name of God, then they become a great leader.

At the end of the day, either you choose God or you don't. What does that leave?

Good mornin'.

People are funny to me.

Everyone thinks they have the answer.

Everyone thinks they have the key.

Most leaders have some arrogance, cockiness, or super confidence.

You must believe in yourself or you're already defeated.

I see and I say people want it their way. People that are flexible make it through life better: they bend, not break.

Everyone has a limit. Mine varies, I go by vibrations.

People say a lot of things, but not many people can speak on my loyalty or love.

Wherever I go, whomever I'm with, I make them comfortable in living. Who makes me comfortable sometimes I bend so much I almost break. I like waking up happy, not looking for what's wrong but what's right.

I don't rest a lot because it's not time.

I'll rest when my job is done.

I'm only special in God's eyes.

To me that's all that matters.

People come and go. God will never leave you.

Hello.

I'm realizing that just because you're not coming to heaven with me doesn't mean you're not coming. You just weren't ready to come with me. It wasn't your time.

Thank you, Lord, for letting me be just who you want me to be.

5/7/18

Good mornin', world.

Be careful. If the devil knows you're one of God's children but you're a runaway child, he's after you. He knows you're lost, and he's going to send his evil after you. He's going to make them look beautiful and shiny, make you feel comfortable with illusion and deceit. He'll send smiling faces. See, God's anointed children can read the signs and go back home where they belong.

Me, I saw I had to be a part of it, and that's when the lord began carrying me.

See, the devil can only control our minds and actions if we allow him. God controls our hearts and souls.

The more I give to God, the less sinfulness I feel.

Devil—lies, deceit, hurt, and pain. A ball of confusion.

God—just the truth, and the truth shall set you free.

Good mornin'.

I'm starting to realize that my thought pattern is slightly different. I really appreciate everything and everybody.

I trust people too much and open up too easily. People hear what they want from me, but when I do, it's a sin.

People make commitments to me and don't keep them.

But let me not keep mine, it's a sin.

As I complain to myself and ask the Lord for help. I'm good.

See, I appreciate a dollar when I don't have it, but when I get an abundance, I forget about that dollar. I'm finally on track.

Thank God.

Every day, I ask God for guidance.

He is placing me where I'm supposed to be.

To me, with growth comes pain.

I am able to sustain more than most.

I'm not better, smarter, or tougher than anyone.

Why can everyone be them and I can accept it, but me being me is so difficult to accept?

I was afraid of being alone.

I'm no longer afraid.

God is the answer.

Ask and you shall receive, but be careful what and how you ask.

6/23/14

Good mornin'.

You know, to me, you can tell good-hearted people from heartless people.

If a good-hearted person gets a little power, they use it to help.

If a heartless person gets it, it's too much, so they change— they want more power, so they lose people.

People seem the same, but if you look into their eyes you can see their soul.

Take for instance when I tell some people about my illness. They will tell me nothing is wrong with me. Now it's two sides; they're either saying it to say "Mac, you're a cool person" or "Ain't nothing wrong with you." They do this or that, and it's mostly the wrong people trying to use me for their best interest.

I have found my way through the maze; now I have to put the puzzle together.

You see, it's not what you have, it's what you do with it.

Like I said, I'm not running. I'm leaving to start anew.

There's a few people I will never leave behind because I was taught never to leave a comrade behind.

Good mornin', world.

The devil is so angry at me now that I truly understand that his job every second of the day, each and every day, is to get the soul of one of God's true children.

So you must move defensively every day to fight the devil. As the saying goes, stay ready so you don't have to get ready.

I'm so glad my mom prayed so hard that she put some prayers on the shelf for me, so when she wasn't physically here, she would protect me still.

Thank you, Mother.

Thank you, Lord.

Good mornin', world.

A lot of old terms have so much meaning.

Your own tongue can be your worst nightmare.

One is the loneliest number.

Be careful what you pray for.

Always protect your heart.

People say so much and do so little.

Manipulators always feel someone is trying to manipulate them.

I'm starting to understand the truth; it's so easy, it's hard to accept sometimes.

The truth is real shit.

A lie is bullshit, so when you can separate real shit from bullshit, you can separate the truth from a lie.

You have to understand that the devil can only use what comes out of your mouth if you believe he can't get in your soul.

A lot of people say I have an excuse for everything.

To me, I have a reason for most things.

Throw it back at them. They never have an excuse.

I'm getting tired. Time to relax and enjoy my accomplishments that are coming.

I thank you, Lord.

People play with you and don't even know it. Sad.

5/31/18

Good mornin', world.

To me, unless we are born with a disability, we are equal.

Disabilities come in many forms; they're physical, mental, and spiritual.

Being able to admit and accept your disability makes the difference.

Accepting starts the process. You begin working on the problem. Determination and motivation is a key component in making it better.

The devil works on our spiritual disability.

Knowledge of the Lord is our only weapon.

Good mornin', world.

Sometimes, the human part of us takes over, and our sensitivity takes over, such as the passing of someone we love dearly.

We forget that by walking with the Lord our savior, we have eternal life.

Death only comes to our physical being.

Think about when we truly know that when the person is going home, there's no more pain and suffering.

It's the true meaning of no worries.

Think about what's best for the one we love.

Good mornin', world.

You know what, I'm realizing that all my life, there have been so many people that I love (that's because I love everyone) trying to point out what I do wrong instead of what I do right.

How can a man go through so much for others, always sharing and caring, and yet gets persecuted? How can a person share all his blessings with everyone and be put down by so many?

How can a person come to save everyone and get betrayed by so many?

I can kind of feel what Jesus went through.

Our father who art in heaven.

If you don't know what a man is, how can you find one?

If you don't know who God is, how can you find him?

As I move with God, life gets clear?

Check yourself.

Make sure you're walking with God, not the devil.

Thank you, Lord, for the light.

Be careful. Even when it looks like I'm losing, I'm really winning.

To me, everyone sees what I do for others, and very few people see what I do for them.

I have no more insecurities. Do you?

If it's not the whole truth, then it's a damn lie.

Good mornin', world.

What makes a person feel privileged in life but put so little into life?

People are always saying what someone else doesn't do or isn't doing.

While they themselves aren't doing anything or are doing very little.

So many people talk like things are so easy. I can do this, I get that—most of those types of people hardly do anything but talk.

I'll tell you, talking is one of the easiest things most people can do nowadays. So many people moving their lips but saying nothing and not being serious.

I'm starting to get new real friends, ones that help me let go of the past while holding on.

What I mean by that is I mostly would hold onto the hurtful part of my past when I had so much good and happy parts to hold onto.

I was very unbalanced, which made me unstable.

Always remember that what you put into anything is what you get out of it.

Why are people always trying to get over on people that truly try and help them?

Hey.

As I start taking life a little more slowly and seriously, I've always liked being a clown when I'm trying to make friends as I always have just about all my life.

The only time I would have bad and hard times is when I would bring them upon myself.

To me, all my life, I've fought good and evil within myself, it seemed I would let evil win most of the time.

It's just that my mother wouldn't give up on me, and my dad let me go for a minute so I could get what I always wanted so bad.

Be careful what you ask for.

I never got a chance to apologize to my father for the disrespect I gave him for no reason.

I always got choices, and I would always choose the negative because it looked positive to me.

When I left home, I was confused and had no guidance.

I lived in my world, so what I did was right to me.

I stopped listening.

That means I stopped learning.

My mother and I always tried to help the unfortunate.

My dad made everyone help themselves unless you were his.

I'm going to start listening. I've always been watching.

I'm going to let the good take over and put the evil in remission.

I've let negativity go.

I tried to explain unbalanced. I'm off the chain because I'm confused.

I'm balanced and I would like to stay this way.

Thank you, Lord.

———∞∞∞———

5/11/18

Good afternoon.

The devil is a conniving, twisted entity, and I got to watch him play.

The biggest weapon that he uses is the heart.

He's been using my heart against me since I left home on my journey.

I talk so much, I confused the devil with what comes out of my mouth.

I've been seeing the light; I just kept wearing sunglasses.

I've been feeling the pain; I just kept numbing it and putting a band aid on a wound that needed stitches. Expecting disrespect when I can't stand being disrespected or disrespecting others.

The end of my road is coming, and it's going to be beautiful.

Good mornin', world.

Lord, why are the streets trying to hold onto me? Then again, why would they want to let me go?

When I was in the streets, within reason, I could get any illegal thing you wanted: drugs, guns, grenades, contracts.

I could call on the fury of hell, and I would get it, but my mother kept praying, probably asking the Lord what she did wrong when what she was doing was keeping me alive.

So when she passed, someone very close told me she transferred the energy of her heart and soul (which is her spirit) to me. That was too much good the devil tried to fight. He needed to keep my soul, actually. He never got my soul just because I never dropped or lost my mustard seed of faith.

Energy never dies.

Faith is what keeps me alive.

———— ∞∞∞ ————

Good mornin'.

When I look back, I'm not so angry at the world anymore.

I feel I kept so much anger because I was living a double life.

I was working for the devil and the Lord at the same time.

That's why one minute I loved the world and the next minute I hated the world, but there was always that 10 percent that I loved internally no matter what. I just made some bad choices. In fact, it was only 10 percent of the 10 percent that was real.

Each time God saw the devil's soldiers overpowering me, he would send just one of my guardians to me because one of my angels are equivalent to ten of the devil's best.

See, all I need is to feel comfortable going into battle.

I need to know for sure that you won't leave me just like you know for sure without a doubt I would never leave you.

That's why, as I say, the devil can't stand me because he just knew he had a sucker.

The Lord gave me the ability to trick the devil.

Because of me being so naive to the streets.

You know the sayin'

Never give a sucker an even break.

Thank you, Lord.

Remember, everyone is worth saving.

Faith.

Good mornin', world.

Be careful in these streets, one lie can change your whole life.

For instance, a young lady says you raped them, or someone says you mess with children, or you're a snitch.

Since so much of that is going on, just the accusation changes how people look at you. Even when you're found innocent, people still look at you with doubt.

The devil uses your tongue as his tool. The deeper you get in the streets, the more the devil has control.

Since he knows the Bible backward and forward.

He'll trick you into thinking you're walking with God, when all the time he's leading you to destruction. Without God, we can't win against the devil.

Having that mustard seed of faith is like having a life raft in the middle of the ocean. You can't see any rescue or any land.

You just ran out of food and water, you're panicking, then you calm down for just a minute and you call to the Lord. You bow your head and close your eyes, you get on your knees in that raft. You ask, "Father, where are you?" and when you open your eyes, there are boats all around you.

Thank you, Lord.

3/16/18

Good mornin', world.

Remember when our parents seemed to be so mean and tough on us or we thought they were? Remember, spare the rod, spoil the child.

Or when we had a teacher that we thought was tough on us, when really they saw potential in us that we didn't know we had? Or a coach that drilled us (it seemed like) more than anyone else? Seems like he's always on us or something.

As youth, we don't understand. As we mature, it becomes clear. To me, knowledge and wisdom are spiritual. As we humble ourselves to our Lord and Savior,

Things become clearer. Our choices become better.

We start getting this glow.

Our thoughts are positive, our path gets straighter and narrower.

We become more confident in ourselves knowing God is always with us.

You start remembering things you could've sworn you forgot (knowledge).

You start reasoning more, make better decisions, taking more time (wisdom).

When you have God, being afraid is not in your vocabulary.

Stepping out on faith becomes an everyday thing.

None of us know for sure what lies in front of us.

What we do know, our choices have a lot to do with our outcome.

Just trust and believe.

Good mornin', world.

See, you can't rush life, you must take your time.

Me, the time I turned twelve is when I started going in the wrong direction.

To me, the devil uses what comes out of your mouth while God uses what comes out of your heart and soul.

You have to be careful with dream and blessing jumpers.

Those are like what a street person would call a car hop or a user.

They come and try and take over your dreams and blessings, twist what you say, try and make you feel bad about your dreams and blessings, persuade you into giving them everything that's yours and then treat you like shit.

Then try and make you look stupid with yours.

The devil looks for your weakness: sex, money, jewelry, attention.

Even the best can get caught up.

It's a dog-eat-dog world, period.

Being humble and meek will show you so much.

When you're quiet and in the back, no one pays too much attention to you, so they are revealing who they are.

So as you move to the front, you know who is who.

Be careful when you ask God to reveal because a lot of times it's going to hurt very bad.

Always remember: God never tries to hurt or embarrass his children.

Stay out of them streets if you can.

Only a few make it out alive.

Follow the light to come out of the darkness.

Thank you, Lord.

We must understand: anger is a weakness. It can throw you off. It makes you out of control, off the chain.

The more control we have of ourselves, the better choices we'll make.

Knowledge is key.

God is the answer.

Good mornin', world.

Have you ever noticed that some people want so much control? If you allow them, they'll try and tell you what, where, and how to act, how to talk, and how to dream.

They'll try and take over how you think and talk. They start seeing what your blessings are, and that's when you must be careful.

That means they're after your heart and soul—the two main things in keeping your faith.

Only God's seasoned soldier can battle them.

If you run into them, don't be afraid to ask for help.

Don't let pride and ignorance stop you.

Always remember, you have comrades. Trust is so major.

I was a fool. I tried to trust everyone. Be careful.

A closed mouth, open ears, and a pure heart and soul will get you through it.

That's called believing.

Rich.

Good mornin', world.

I'm starting to understand: rich isn't money; it's spiritual.

When you give God the lead, you're headed for riches beyond your imagination. You get rid of fear and confusion.

You feel as though you're getting weak when you're getting stronger.

You lose people you never would have thought.

Some you keep because they have a chance.

A person can lead you to the pearly gates.

Only you can get yourself through.

God is the answer.

Good mornin', world

It's not the world that has a problem; it's the people in it.

The people start feeling privileged, and very few people want to take responsibility for what they do.

When things go good, everyone will claim that, but when it goes bad, fingers start pointing.

Someone said, "Mac, when people hit the lottery or win people wish that was them, when people get ill or something bad happens, no one wants to claim that."

As I look at myself, I had begun living in a box accepting wooden nickels.

Finding excuses for others.

There are a lot of sicknesses in the world—mental, physical, and spiritual.

The world is so twisted and manipulated now.

God, as you show me the light, the darkness is always trying to hold on.

Good mornin', world.

To me, you have to go through life to understand life.

Us—the value of life dissipates, it's starting to confuse people, especially our youth.

I remember when respect was an automatic given, when honor and pride was mandatory.

Now, each person has their own analogy of respect, honor, loyalty, and love.

How can a person that's not that teach someone to be that?

Example, how can someone teach a boy to be a man when they don't know themselves?

Like I said before, if you're living in a box, how can you know what's outside that box?

Trying to get out of that box is going to bring some joy and pain.

So the quicker you find your lane, the easier your life can be.

No one is better than anyone, it's our choices.

Always God first, then you.

This world is becoming confused.

Only those who truly believe can get through it.

Thank you, Lord.

12/30/17

Good mornin', world.

To me, being one of God's soldiers isn't easy.

Every day you go through training, knowing that every day the devil is after you.

Sometimes you have to even get captured so you can find out his plans.

Only a true believer can make it out alive.

As long as you keep that mustard seed of faith, you can survive.

See, a mustard seed is so small that you can easily lose it with all the fake gold, money, fame, and power the devil can seemingly give you.

It's a hell of a battle. If you can make it through that, God knows you're ready.

Good mornin', world.

In my opinion, when these streets get in your blood, it starts slowly enveloping you. You start letting your guard down. You start letting the glitter (fake gold) become real. You start thinking the streets are your friend when really they're your enemy.

No matter what walk of life you're in, there's jealousy and envy, but it's nothing like street envy and jealousy.

You become a bully in a way, taking the weak's possessions so you can look stronger.

Nowadays, everyone calls each other bitches like it's the thing to do, males and females.

To me, we are losing our own value as men and women—a lot of people that don't do anything feel someone owes them everything.

I always talked about money—90 percent of people with no drive always take it as I'm boasting.

God and my mother's prayers tried to make my life easy, but I preferred the devil's way. It looked easier when you're heading for disaster.

In general, most people bring up money when I bring it up. I'm told, "All you do is bring up your money." When others bring it up, it's cool.

I'm going to a spiritual place soon.

Me and all my discrepancies, all my blessings, and all my sins.

All my life, people complain about my money, but only a few ever turned it down.

People are so funny, that's why I'm so silly, because people make me laugh.

If you think these streets are the answer, think again. God is the answer.

12/3/17

Good mornin', world.

I think the only reason I made it through my journey was because of my mother's and father's prayers and every other person that said a prayer for me. I just think my parents had a little more impact only because they were my parents. They created me. My mother conceived me, carried me, nurtured me, and guided me. Then I was born. They fed me, clothed me, sheltered me, protected me, and tried to guide me. They put up with my mess—disciplined me, never abused me mentally or physically, never allowed me to be in harm's way, never tried to send me into this cold world. In fact, they tried their best to keep me away from it.

They saw a little insanity or difference in me. They tried to hold on to me, but the streets started calling me, testosterone started bubbling—the devil was getting ahold of me. But what I didn't know was that my parents had anointed me before I was born, so no weapon formed against me shall prosper. Now, I'm sure most parents do this, but I positively and without a doubt know this of mine.

Now, let my journey begin. For now, we'll just say I'm Mac. I was born in Hartford, Connecticut in a place we call Hooterville. Actually, it was a pretty tight-knit community. I was born January of '58 to Bertha and James. I had two adopted sisters: sister one, who was there before me, and sister two, who came around the second grade and stayed only a few years.

Sister one was shy, naive, a little low in self-esteem, and a little afraid, while sister two was arrogant, cocky, outgoing, and knowledgeable about the streets young. Me, I was in the middle before sister two came. I was similar to sister one, when sister two came. She started bringing out the other me. At first, I would get bullied on, always wanting to fight back but was afraid, feeling all the time I didn't have any backup when all the time I had some of the baddest backup I could ask for—my dad (but what little boy wants to run home and get their dad?). I never saw anyone disrespect my dad nor did I see him disrespect anyone. I saw him move the crowd a few times. Also, I had my mother, she would have taken a rational approach. She would say, "Let's go talk to the parents and the principal, let's pray on it." (What little boy wants his mom bringing him to the people's house or up to the school for you to tell on someone?) Praying on it, in a child's mind, isn't going to work. I'm a child, I don't know any better, so I endured it.

At first, good grades, quiet, respectful (boring).

Hanging out with the so-called nerds.

Then sister two came.

She'd fight anyone. If you were her elder, she'd give you respect, but don't push her too far. She started bringing the tough crew, the whoop ass crew, the popular crew. Some of them would watch my back. Sister two would always have my back.

Good mornin', world.

To me, sometimes people are so busy trying to make a person like they want them to be, that they can't see the person for who they really are. Without good, there would be no bad. Without right, there would be no wrong. What would the world be without negative and positive? Now imagine life without God.

3/23/18

Hello.

My father was such a strong man—the strength he gave me is what enabled me to walk through hell.

So my mother's wisdom and guidance, my father's strength and his being a true man, and their combined faith brought me back here which is the path to heaven.

Thank you, parents.

Good mornin', world.

Life is so changing—every minute, something is changing.

Take Shark Tank. It's been on for years, and in every program, three or four people come at them with an idea for them to be loaned some money and get a partnership in their idea.

Everyone wants a part of the money. No one on Shark Tank's panel need any money, but they all started from humble beginnings. Also, it's the true meaning of the rich get richer.

That's the same thing as getting rich with the Lord.

God sends someone rich with his wisdom and spirit to make us rich in his spirit. Less people are jumping on that train.

Society is trying to get rid of God—can't pray in school, can't bring a Bible, but you literally can bring a gun.

We aren't safe in school, church, your home—where can God's children go?

Look at all the chaos in the world. Do we see that?

Are we really paying attention to the signs?

See, they can only try and get rid of God, the nonbelievers. God can easily get rid of us.

Pay attention and believe.

Good mornin', world.

Remember the saying "Say what you mean and mean what you say"? I remember when my word was my bond. You could almost set your clock on my word back then. When I look back, every drug I sold and used, almost every mean and disrespectful thing I've done in my life has come back and slapped me in my face hard and firm.

People put up a front so much, a lot of people that act too hard have an inner fear of something.

To me, a lot of people are afraid to step out on faith for fear of the unknown. We have to venture into the unknown to make it known. See, whatever God doesn't want us to know, we'll never find out. He wants us to venture out to find out certain things. We must realize God's fearless soldiers must keep not being afraid. And even when they're afraid, realize the devil has fearless soldiers as well, ones that use darkness as their main weapon.

See, the only thing that can beat darkness is the light. Remember, as a kid, most of us couldn't stand the darkness too long. Somebody hurry up and turn on some light. The Earth is the devil's playground. He uses everything in his arsenal to keep us in the dark. See, the only thing the devil and his soldiers fear are God and his soldiers. The only thing God's soldiers fear is God himself.

When you truly let God in, you start being less and less afraid.

Good mornin', world.

We always need to pay attention when we don't understand something—don't be afraid to ask.

Most of us know what a dumb question is.

Then why would we go the hard way to get the answer the roundabout way (we call it) when we personally can go directly to the source for the answer?

Remember the game in school where you start at one end of the room, say one phrase, and by the time it gets to the other end, it's a completely different phrase?

So that made me always think: "Why would I start at the end of the class and get a lie when I'm capable of going to the head of the class and getting the truth?"

God is the answer. God is the head, devil is the tail.

1/16/18

Dear Lord,

I thank you for all you have allowed me to see, endure, and overcome.

You have given me personal testimonies and positioned me to see others' testimonies. You put my soulmate, my growth, and responsibility in my life.

You put a reason back in my life.

You are taking me and my mate to a spiritual level.

You are giving me all my strength back.

Lord, I never would have made it without you.

Only Bertha Mae Gibson and James David McGarrah could have created me.

I truly went through life not giving a damn about too much of nothing when I truly had so much to be thankful for.

Good mornin', world.

God is revealing to me everything I'm needing to learn. Greed, deceit, lies—all things I didn't even realize I had in myself at one time. Not many people take the time to really look at themselves. They're too busy trying to find fault in everyone else.

To me, the devil is always trying to trick a person with lies and deceit. To me, God watches, and when the devil thinks he has you, God intervenes.

This upsets the devil a lot of times. When you upset the devil, he tells the truth about himself. To me, most good people see the good in me and most bad people see the bad in me. To me, most of the time, I see the real in people now.

Thank you, Lord.

Good mornin', world.

Sometimes we as humans judge some of us though we don't mean to. It's just human nature.

See, God builds each individual for the task he has predestined for us. The only thing we don't know is when he's going to call on us.

To me, we get tested every day to make sure whenever he calls on us we'll be ready. Now, when he's preparing you to be a soldier, it's intense training. Like trying to be a Navy Seal, one hundred try out and seven make it. For God's soldiers, one thousand try out and only one can make it.

See, the devil will get high tech on you. All these things to make life easy so you can get lazy—all this fame, money, power, you can't take any of it with you.

God's soldiers keep an open heart, and that's the mustard seed of faith.

God knows even a soldier needs relief sometimes—soldiers never get much rest.

God's soldiers are built to last like a Tonka truck. So you, as a soldier, never give up. That's why God knows exactly when to send you relief. God never makes a mistake.

To me, each person has a predestined task. If, during our everyday trials and tribulations, God sees we can't handle it, you are still his child. You just can't be a soldier.

See, everyone can't be on the battlefield—just as long as you are a part of his army.

———⊂⊃———

11/25/2017

Good mornin', world.

Each individual sees life through their own eyes. In some countries, the stuff we throw away for trash would be a luxury for them. All I'm saying is, sometimes we, as human beings, take a lot for granted or feel we're owed something. As someone once said, "One man's trash is another man's treasure." Or "nothing comes to a sleeper but a dream."

To me, if you don't make forward progress, you can't move forward (going backward or standing still). How could you move forward?

People say, what's wrong with thinking outside the box or the norm? This is how all inventions are born and progress is made.

To me, all people have something selfish about them, whether it's mental, physical, or spiritual.

Most people stagnate themselves by living in a box. Don't put a limit on yourselves. Sometimes boundaries must be broken to keep moving.

To me, that's what steppin' out on faith is. Believing in God first and foremost, while also believing in yourself. A mind is a terrible thing to waste. We must listen to learn. Pay attention to your surroundings. Humble yourselves. Sometimes it's rough. Actually, no one is better than anyone. It's mostly the choices we make with the free will God gave us. So stop blaming others and start making better choices.

To me, so many people want to be more than what they are when just being who you are will do.

To me, there's a certain type of people who want to take me down a notch because they think I think I'm all that. Some of them love me, some of them deep down inside have something against me because it seems one way when it's really another. Instead of coming with me, they want me to stay or come back with them.

I'm a true believer, so I continue steppin'.

Yeah, though I walk through the valley of the shadows of death, I shall fear no evil for thou art with me. Thy rod and thy staff shall comfort me, I prepareth a table in the presence of mine enemy.

My quest for knowledge is returning. I've seen the dark side. Let there be light.

If people love people for who they are, why do people attempt to change a person to who they want them to be while they feel they can remain the same?

To me, life is exciting and fun. To others, life is serious and hard.

Who would you rather be?

5/13/18

Good mornin', Lord.

You are the light at the end of the tunnel.

When I follow the light you shine on me, it becomes brighter and wider.

The darkness becomes smaller and smaller. The darkness had consumed me. The only light I saw were street lights. Not the moon and the stars, sometimes not even the sun.

As I walk into God's light, I'm finding the right road to take, and the road is getting clearer.

Thank you, Lord.

5/16/17

Good mornin', world.

As I see myself really leaving the streets, I understand why I had to hang on to my past. So as I put my puzzle together, it was a map to completely get me out of hell, so when I come to the fork in the road, I know which path to take.

When you truly let God be your savior, the things he shows you, the wealth he bestows upon you.

Our father who art in heaven.

Sometimes we fear the wrong things in life. Remember, as a baby, all you knew was love. You didn't know the difference between right and wrong. Good and bad, pretty and ugly, nice and mean.

You're just full of God. Remember.

Good mornin' once again.

You know, to me, all prayers are powerful and heard, but a mother's sincere prayers for their babies no matter how old are the most powerful. Their undying love for theirs has a special place. "Do as I ask," sayeth the Lord, "and I will bless your children." Being a real mother is one of the hardest jobs, for me.

Now, let's not leave out being a real father, because you're always around no matter where you physically are, providing and protecting your family to the best of your ability. Being a real father is the second hardest job for me— with the mother or not, you're still supposed to do your job.

We're human, we make mistakes. Does that mean we give up? No. That means man up, big guy.

Good mornin', world.

The Lord is taking me to heights I couldn't have imagined. All the pain I caused others, but all I could bring up is what someone did to me. So the Lord made me lay in each bed that I made, but it was a little harder, a little thornier.

All the disrespect I gave to others I got slapped in the face with.

I've passed my tests and asked for forgiveness in a real way. Like I said, we must be careful what we ask for, and the tricky part is how we ask for it.

We actually only get one mother, one father, and one God. Sometimes we can substitute a mother or a father, but we cannot substitute our Lord and Savior. Mother, thank you for that mustard seed of faith.

Father, thank you for the strength. Parents, thank you for my endurance.

Lord, thank you for your mercy.

In your name.

Lord, Amen.

Hello.

When you think it can't get any better when you're walking with God, it just keeps getting better.

<hr/>

Good mornin' again.

People are a trip. Everyone has issues, only a few people can admit them.

People have to hold back who they really are so no one will know their weakness, or hide their fears to make another MF think they're harder, tougher, or whatever.

Everyone puts into their head that their way is right, but the proof is in the pudding.

I say and do what I want. God gave me free spirit.

God let me get weak. I took all kinds of unnecessary abuse, ridicule, and persecution, but this showed me who was real to me and who wasn't.

I was blinded, but my mom served God too well and prayed too hard for the devil to take control of me. I had humbled myself to negative worthless shit when I always had an option.

I allowed myself to get humiliated and belittled by unworthy people.

People can say what they want about me, but I'm not fake, and I'm loyal and mostly honest.

This is the end of the road for me.

The world is full of users. I don't want to be used anymore. People would get my shit and act like they made me.

I make people. I help most people more than they help me, but to them, they've done so much for me.

Anyway, life is getting clearer. Once again, I have no fear. You know you did me wrong. That means it was on purpose. Be careful, because really, I'm off the chain.

People don't understand, they almost released the kraken that's a titan, only another titan has a chance, but most titans get along with me because of respect, not fear.

A true leader always puts him or herself into battle also because they enjoy participating to show that actions speak louder than words.

Well, I'm contained again, but if you did me on purpose, beware. Leave me alone, because next time it will be all bad for you. When I'm angry, fear is not an option.

Later.

Good mornin'.

I used to think I had mean parents who didn't know much about the world.

Keeping me away from all the good stuff.

Insisting I go to school and church.

Respecting my elders no matter what, having principles and morals, keeping me away from anything that could harm me mentally, physically, or spiritually.

Parents' main purpose is to protect, provide, and shelter.

I never didn't have anything, but I was so selfish, I twisted it the way I wanted in my brain. All they did was try and love me to the best of their ability.

I truly understand now—wisdom comes with living and experiencing. I have reaped what I sowed all my life. Always realize life is a cycle.

To me, if you keep letting it go by, you're subject to get confused. You have to find your stop and get off or you might just keep riding lost.

Thank you, Lord, for letting me understand. I sometimes thought people made me who I am when it's you, Lord.

I've had so much pain; I should be numb.

My stop is coming, and I will get off this ride.

Today is my day, given to me by God.

3/3/14

Good mornin'.

When I look back, I lost my mind a long time ago, when I didn't realize where I really came from and started thinking on my own without values or principles.

Never making sure my home was safe, always leaving it open to predators, but I was young, off the chain, and carefree, but curious about hell. So when I left home, I went on a mission to find out what hell was all about. Well, you know me, I had to get to the center of it so I could meet Satan himself. Did I make it?

Now that I've found out what hell was all about, I'm ready to come home, stop fighting, structure, listen, and be quiet, be a good follower so I can be a good leader.

Now, I want to structure so I can be a strong man. I'm on my way to heaven so I can be with my family and for the first time I can be at peace.

There is truly a God, but we must put forth effort to find him. Just truly believe, and he will always be there.

Dwight D. McGarrah Sr.

I've been in the Marine Corps, college, prison, a marriage, and a church. I've been a crackhead, junky, gangbanger, dope dealer, semipimp, shooter, and fighter. I've been off a cliff and down a mountain, but I feared no evil, for thou was with me.

Good mornin', world.

As I reflect on my past and start to let it go and accept why the things for me are the way they are, I can accept them easier. I didn't get punished in the physical realm so harsh. It's the spiritual realm that gets me. I'm really getting it now. When the next blessing comes and presents itself for me to clean up and come anew, I'm going to do just that.

Then I can move on with no worries or regrets.

Thank you, Lord.

2/22/17

Good mornin', world.

Lord, you have given me so many tests so I can have so many testimonies. It's a certain group of people that think I brag and boast when I speak of my failures and accomplishments. I can't help if I made it through life with my brain and my lack of fear. Once I left home, I was on my own.

Yes, my parents looked out for me some, but not much. I really made my own way. Be careful to whom you speak and what you say. People will think yours is theirs. Why do people try and take others' accomplishments?

To me, people that think they're strong get mad upset or whatever because I get and always have gotten mine. To me, people that don't think I deserve mine try and take mine over. The world is getting so corrupt. You don't know who to trust.

Maybe being alone is the answer. For now, the Lord has it where I can do everything I want. I can truly have it my way but my purpose is generosity. Have to really figure this one out. I'm like a wild horse with a free spirit that people always try and catch and tame, but I always escape. Maybe I was born to be free.

Prosperity.

Hello.

To me, prosperity is spiritual, not material. When you give it to God, he will show you what prosperity is.

I had gotten so lost in these streets that I had gotten upside down; instead of coming out of the hole, I was digging myself deeper into the hole.

Once again, I know which way is up, and I'm finally really on my way up.

Good mornin', world.

Dear Lord, thank you for the mercy and wisdom you have bestowed upon me. I've seen and continue to see so much—my journey is becoming clearer. My humility is allowing me to pay better attention to my surroundings, and for my future, understanding and patience are very necessary commodities.

My past actions are becoming relevant in my present and future. Yesterday was a good day, didn't call anyone to gossip or didn't stress about much. God is my answer.

5/9/18

Good mornin', world.

We're born pure and we die pure if we repent.

The only time we don't have any say-so is during our conception and if we get too old to handle our own physical and mental needs.

When we're born, we come out knowing nothing, we start learning the moment we open our eyes.

God makes triple darkness within the woman. Man cannot duplicate triple darkness during our development if our parents are putting bad chemicals such as drugs and alcohol in their system; it affects the fetus.

It's a fact that if a parent that reads to their unborn child, the child's mind starts developing. What is read makes a big difference also.

Everyone makes bad choices, and God knows we do. Our choices are what make us imperfect. God is the only entity that's never going to make a bad choice.

If we let God lead us beside the still waters, we'll be coming to peace.

When we can wake up in God's peace, we know we're on our way to heaven.

When we give it to God, it's truly like being born again. We have nothing to hide.

Since our hearts and souls belong to God, what allows the devil to get them?

Can we give them away? Can we sell them? Are some people born without a heart and soul?

How can two identical twins be so different, one as pure in goodness as can be and the other be pure evil?

Forgive us, Father.

Good mornin', world.

When we realize that we are God's greatest creations of all his creations, we feel special. How can we not? We look at all his creations—the air, the universe, the ocean, the mountains, valleys, and all the in-betweens, and out of that, each individual to themselves is his greatest creation.

Good mornin', world.

Why is there so much anger in the world? Why do so many people control or actually think they control? There are two major control powers: good and bad.

Sometimes what our intentions are in the beginning changes. Say for instance you open a place for the homeless. At first, it's really coming from your heart. You work hard every day putting fliers up, going on radio and TV, and then people start donating merchandise and funds. Prosperity is starting to show quickly.

You never thought it would be like this—the money starts pouring in, and you start to want more for yourself. At first, you buy nice good-quality stuff for the people, and you buy yourself a nice watch that's a little expensive. Now, you need a ring and a chain to go with it. Now, you need a nice car and a big house. You start hanging out with a different crowd, the kind of crowd you always thought you wanted to hang with. You start drinking, smoking.

Letting your facility go down, you forget about the people and only think about yourself.

Now, on the other hand, you take someone high-power, cocky, already thinking that if you don't make three hundred thousand a year, you're beneath them. But they get this project in the inner city. They start meeting people that just got bad breaks and never got a chance to show their potential. They start realizing that people are people.

Now, they open a facility in the inner city and really start helping the unfortunate.

Lord, I thank you.

12/13/2013

Good mornin', world.

To me, a lot of people who don't feel they have anything to lose and have low self-esteem don't care about a person working hard, sacrificing, and going through hell to get somewhere in life. Making calculated moves, good choices.

Then, one bad decision can jeopardize everything you worked hard for—scrapping, scuffling, headaches, pain, and suffering.

Then, when you lose everything, the nothing people move on trying to find someone else to try and bring down.

These people don't respect themselves, let alone anyone else.

All these laws to protect the youth, and look how disrespect-ful they are nowadays.

If a youngster disrespects you, you put your hands on them, and they call the police, and you go to jail.

When I was a child, you got hands put on you (a whoopin') by the teacher, the principal, and the neighbor, and when you got home. Then, if the police were called, the child was leaving.

Now, if the police come, you don't know who is going to jail. You must be wiser with your choices, the more you accomplish.

It's easy to get into trouble and so hard to get out of it. So you must think it out. There's always a way to accomplish what you need done without making a bad choice.

Pray on it, and you'll get the answer.

You know, I see most people try to blame others for their fuck-ups. I am a prime example. I have more excuses in a week than the average person has in a lifetime.

It's hard to believe anything or anybody nowadays because it's so much bullshit. People trading horses in the middle of the stream.

Me, I'm fucked up in the head. My baby boy is in trouble, and I can't save him. I always save my babies. My journey is uncertain now, but it's in God's hands.

I completely trust him and can't ever doubt him. Whatever he does, it's for the best.

Thank you, Lord, for everything you have done for me and mine.

12/26/2017

Good mornin'.

Listening requires no talking. I talk too much.

Lord, you are the only identity that's 100 percent.

Lord, you never make a mistake. You never take back what you give.

You already know before it happens. The more I give my soul to you, the clearer and more positive life gets.

Lord, only you have the final say-so in everything.

You give life. Let us make choices when you are in charge. Even the worst decision you make turns out right.

God can clean it right up.

When you give it to God, he will show you the light, because God is the light.

Every day, he breathes the breath of life into each individual.

Sometimes we can't see the forest for the trees.

Nowadays most people think they're on point.

Playing with God is a sin.

Just be thankful for what we got.

4/27/2017

Good mornin', world.

Most people in general feel their way is the only way, rich or poor.

Some think tough is it, but the meek shall inherit the Earth.

Some think having a lot of money is it. Money won't get you into heaven.

Some think power is the answer. Nothing is more powerful than God.

To me, it's putting your trust and love in God and knowing your relationship with him because God is one-on-one. There are billions of people on Earth, yet still, God has time to deal with each individual one at a time.

Believing in God wholeheartedly, then believing in yourself, your choices, and your actions normally dictates your outcome. To me, there is always the 10 percent which against all odds. They make it. Each person makes it their own way. Some things were similar, but each is different.

Success, to me, is what you think it is. Some people may think rich is success, some may think being the best in something is success, some may think just being able to feed your family and pay your bills is success.

For me, coming closer to God, knowing who I am, is success.

Dear Lord,

As I surrender to you, you make my life so clear. As I start to understand myself, it makes it easier to understand others. As I get older and wisdom approaches, the mountain reveals so much. I've been doing my job all my life. As you set me up for retirement, my past doors are closing and new ones are opening.

I am learning, truly, what doesn't kill you makes you stronger. I've talked so much and told so much that I know I must prepare for battle. It's time for my dreams once again. Real shit and bullshit.

Why do I always end up in the same square one?

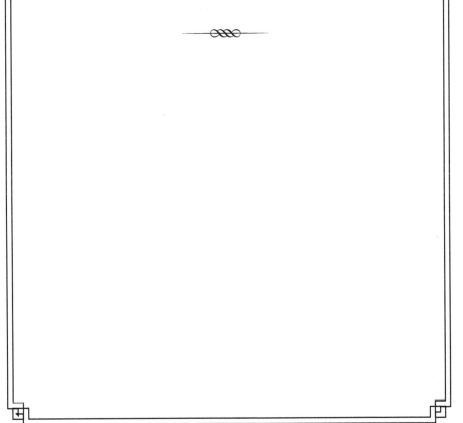

Hello.

I notice money is so tight that people will do almost anything to get it. Good people will connive, some will even sell their soul. Money can make you forget.

See, these are my thoughts. What I think and feel. No one took a bullet for me and I for no one else. People can say and will say anything because I do to get what I want.

My point is, one plus one equals two in every country, continent, wherever. There are people that can add and subtract.

People always or mostly say, "If I had what you had, I'd do this." There are millionaires in all fields, all colors. Some work hard, some it was given to them, some are smart, some not-so-intelligent.

People always saying shit, man. Change what they want, the only things that never change are God's laws, man. Changes birthdays, historical events, he tries to change God's laws, but God is in your soul and heart. They can't take it away.

Let me reiterate: to me, if I want to go left and you want to go right, to me, the only way everyone gets their way is to separate and go each other's way.

To me, it's the small things that show your heart. I really got foolish. I got hurt so bad that it made me regress. I started trying to buy love and friends like I did when I was a child.

When I debate about something, that means I believe what I'm saying or doing is right. Just like you think you're right. What makes me wrong for thinking I'm correct until proven wrong?

What's so farfetched about that?

I've been a sucker for women all my life, but I never played with my money. I'm letting people get me for my money. People owe me and act like I owe them.

―⦅∞⦆―

9/25/14

Hey.

You know the saying, "A fool and his or her money are soon parted."

To me, most people are users in their own way no matter what it's for. Money can make a good person bad. You can actually buy people in a way if you have money.

Your mind has to be strong and you have to be very observant, and you have to listen and speak less so you can hear. To me, you must use all your senses, sometimes individually, but most of the time altogether.

It's nothing like an old fool.

Shit, these last six years, I have gotten very weak and very foolish.

I wasn't listening to the people that cared about me, just for me.

I wanted, like I said, to be impressive, but to who?

I had no reasoning. The kid in me always wanted to share with whomever I felt needed it. I just made a lot of bad choices.

My negative side has been going away rapidly this last year since my mom passed.

I felt I got used some, but the lessons I learned in these past five years are priceless.

7/2/14

My belief as a gangster is never going to stay broke long. That's what makes him or her a gangster. They are truly a go-getter by whatever means necessary.

But they have codes and morals that true gangsters stick to and will die for.

I'm truly getting tired now, and it's getting time for real. When I leave, I'm not running, just moving on. So stop trying to make me feel bad or sad for my choices. Do what you would be doing if I wasn't in your life.

Don't use my love and heart as a rug to wipe your feet on.

I let you make your decisions, so let me make mine.

I don't know what had gotten into me accepting so much bullshit, but now I want real shit.

Not mad at anyone, just disappointed in myself. I'm truly blessed for my parents to have put God in me. The devil knows, and the Bible too. He was once one of God's closest angels.

Always keep your guards up and pay attention—there are always signs.

6/14/14

Hey.

I see people limit their dreams and therefore limit themselves.

I see that money controls more than what they think.

Everyone wants money, but won't really do what it takes to get it.

Anyone that knows me nineteen and better, that's been around, knows I made a few million.

So trust me, one or two million is not a dream.

To those who never had it, it's a dream.

Every successful entrepreneur had a dream, followed it, worked hard at it, and accomplished it.

Even though I'm sure they got persecuted and laughed at, they didn't care.

Einstein was so brilliant, they thought he was crazy. The Wright brothers flying, I bet, but did they care?

The law of relativity. Airplanes. We have to open our minds. We only use 8–10 and 12 percent of our mind. So why not dream and stimulate your mind more.

I see I have to go alone, pursue my dream, come back, and get those I want with me. Every day is bringing something new, and I thank God.

Good mornin'.

You know, the devil is so knowing, he'll trick you into letting him give you a number so he can take away your name. That's an old song from secret agent man.

A secret is meant for only you to know. As for me, I have no secrets, so nothing can come back and haunt me.

To me, the most hurtful thing in life is to give your all financially, physically, mentally, and most of all spiritually, and not be appreciated by others. It may not mean anything, but to me it means everything. Me, I'm love, I'm pure, and I'm real, but that's to me.

To me, I'm God's greatest creation. I got that from a prayer.

1/23/18

Good mornin', world.

Life is full of anything you want it to be. Joy and happiness, or pain and sorrow.

Always remember, negative and positive complement each other. Like day and night.

To me, what good would one be without the other?

You need the intellectuals to figure shit out. You need the laborers to do the job, and you need the supervisors, the managers, so on and so forth in between.

In life, if you get a solid team where everyone knows their positions and stay in their own lane, so much can get done.

United we stand.

Divided we fall.

4/8/17

Good mornin'.

It's actually a beautiful day. I'm starting to really figure shit out.

Because I tell my issues, and I'm so kind and gullible that it makes me look kind of stupid, it seems like very few people actually listen about my journey or who my mom and dad were. How educated and faithful to the Lord my mother was.

For me, I didn't need much education in those streets, so that side of me slowed down. Since I'm actually off the chain, I would just act or react to shit instead of thinking them out. That's because that's the mentality that I had to have to get through this journey. I've done things, and I've heard and seen things. I retained it all, but would only use bits and pieces. The kid in me.

Now I somewhat think on what I do. Soon, I will be thinking the whole scenario out using this brain I was given. That means use common sense and start building my educational side back up.

Thank you, Lord.

———✄———

11/27/17

Good mornin', world.

It feels good to be able to kick back and thank God for all he has carried or guided us through.

Man will always let you down in some shape or fashion. God won't ever let you down. I guess I looked for approval from people for so long. It's hard to let go.

For me, as long as I did or do that, I will stay confused, so now I listen and even respond.

At the end of the day, for me, when it all matters, I know God has me, so I sleep good and wake up happy just because.

I truly have everything I need for success. It's on me now. Time to stop talking, that's going to be hard for me.

I'm starting to see how different but similar I am from most people I deal with—not better, just different. God belongs to everyone who truly believes in him, not just me.

I haven't done one thing in life that hasn't been done before. There are just a few things I've done that people I know haven't done. I'm sure everyone has a couple of friends that would loan them a couple of thousands if they had it. I just have a couple of friends that had it.

---

Be careful who you'll risk your life for.
Watch out for Mr. Greed and Mr. Selfish.
Last question before I go.
What does "off the chain" mean?
I thought it meant "Do what you want when you want."
When I'm happy, my off the chain is silly and childish.
When I'm angry, my off the chain is kill, destroy.
So without balance, either-or. Now I'm balanced.
Good for me, and some of y'all.
So at the end of the day, it does matter how you get there.
If you go the right way, you can relax and enjoy (go to heaven).
But if you go the wrong way, you'll burn in hell.

# About the Author

The author, Dwight McGarrah, grew up in a working-class neighborhood where there was great pride in homeownership, strength in community, and an extreme focus on God and church. His mother was a highly educated schoolteacher who taught in some of the most prestigious schools in Connecticut. His father also held a supervisory position in the school system. The author's parents raised him on the ways of taking the right path, but as he entered in adulthood, he decided to take the path most traveled and ended up in the wilderness for some thirty-plus years. During his years in the wilderness, he lived a life of lying, cheating, stealing, selling drugs, and using drugs. The wilderness, with all its negativity, also awakened Dwight to the fact that God will never leave you or forsake you.

CPSIA information can be obtained
at www.ICGtesting.com
Printed in the USA
FFHW022100270819
54586143-60265FF